Poetic Agony

Poetic Agony

CYNTHIA A. THOMAS

PALMETTO
PUBLISHING
Charleston, SC
www.PalmettoPublishing.com

Hardcover ISBN: 9798822947702
Paperback ISBN: 9798822947719

Merciful God

I thank the Lord for answering my prayers
He has giving me everything I ask for in my darkest hour while in
despair you love me so much that you remove me from shame and pain,
Self love and self respect is what I have gained

Amen!

Contents

CYNTHIA A. THOMAS

MARTIN LUTHER KING

No disrespect Dr. King I love you dearly,
but we need to sit down, my guy, pay attention I need you to hear me.
It's 2024 and things have not yet changed
Can I ask you one question: where in the hell did you get your **enigmatic**
dream from?
Are you sure that the dream was from God
no disrespect Dr. king but your dream have left African-Americans in agony
mourning from the same scars
Begging to be treated equally begging for the damn shackles to be removed
from their feet
Honestly, I feel like we should have not integrated
Before integration our communities was filled with black entrepreneurs
but now our community is filled with dirty fiends and nasty whores
no goals no ambition and alcohol abusers
can't help but to think it has something to do with your dream
wish you were here so I could better prove it
Malcom X looked at you like a fool
could his opinion about integration be more like the truth?

CYNTHIA A. THOMAS

LIGHT AFTER DARKNESS

The hardships of my life is like trying to find light at the end of the tunnel
I'm super lost in this world out of mind out of sight
As I walk through this dark tunnel of life, the aroma attacks my
nostrils sort of like the guy with the mask waiting in the alley
out of nowhere he attacks
Extremely Terrified of the fact that I have no sight
Im
Not going out like no sucker I'm going to put up a fight despite
The agony in my feet caused by the over heated pavement If I make it out of
here alive my feet will need major displacement
I made my bed now I
Must lie in
It
Subliminally the tunnel is
The complications of My life
The darkness is my pain, the hot pavement is guilt and shame.
Approaching the light at the end of the tunnel, achievements
confirmedeliminated all fears, everlasting happiness has finally
arrived after all of these years
My experience out of this is
"NonMatter what life throws at you have
faith and don't quit"

CYNTHIA A. THOMAS

NO MAN NO CRY

If you shed a tear you're labeled as being soft if you wear
your emotions on your sleeve then you weak
No Man No Cry No Man No Cry
Hold your head up I'm here to inform you that
You are as strong as a Lion swift as a shark
And mighty as a giant!

If you broke you are labeled as worthless if you not a
thug or a gangster you're label as a lame
No Man No Cry
You are the first creator therefore you are highly favored
You're the Yin to the Yang the gain that comes from the pain
Society judges your credibility but my brother I'm here for you
No Man No Cry No Man No Cry
be yourself my king dry your eyes my brother your worth
is more valuable than gold
Be bold feeling sorry for yourself gets played out and old
No Man No Cry No Man No Cry
Reach your highest potential you deserve everything this world
has to offer after everything you been through
No Man No Cry
Me and my black sister will hold you down we're here by your side
Cry? No, No Man No cry

CYNTHIA A. THOMAS

GOVERNMENT TRAP

"Never will there be another black panther moment"
"We will come up with a modern day slavery"
Mentally destroy them ALL we not going to be choosy
make them think they are winning when in actuality they're losing.
The black man can sit at the table with us
We will use him for some good luck to deliver our message
Resulting in his household being filled with stress and depression
There will never be another black panther moment
It's a must, it's urgent and it's mandatory that we teach them a critical lesson
Mentally enslaved they will search obliviously for a form of heaven
Unable to find happiness let's just comfort them by flooding their
neighborhoods with crack
Lost hope addiction and poverty will result in suicide,
and homicides back to back
Our plan will be accomplished ignoring their pleas and cries
Another black man destroyed now let's laugh at them and wave goodbye
let's quickly benefit from their stupidity and act like we are concerned
Send the black man to prison our number one business
lots of money will be earn
this will create a generation of a broken race who will be ignorant of the
power that has been purposely replace
In their dominant DNA that runs throughout their blood
is why we hate and envy them
Specially made by God wonder why he didn't give us none

cont.

CYNTHIA A. THOMAS

The black women will be left with the responsibility of
raising her children alone
To be rich they will sell their soul
different men will enter in and out of the black woman's home
Take the fathers out of the home, throw them in prison
the minds of their family will be gone
The black women will forget the true meaning of self love
While Yearning praying and pleading for just one hug
with the influences of social media and our co-workers yup the celebrities
the black man's priority is becoming respected as a thug
This mindset will be passed on from generation to generation
High five KKK's for teaching these ignorant NIGGAS a lesson
Again... there will never be another black panther moment
That's all for this session
SINCERELY USA GOVERNMENT

CYNTHIA A. THOMAS

CRACKED

Now here's the veracity
You came to me and introduced yourself as the hell founder
I was petrified at first but I remembered that I had my father
He is he and he's the one and only luminescence in this calamitous
cruel evil disobedient world
After your awkward introduction I fell down on my knees
for I knew that God Would rescue my inner girl
confessing all of my sins crying and praying
until he informed me that he had to kill me
In order to rebuild and remove the wickedness that lies within my soul
He made a statement about dismembering me
I was a little confused at that statement but god is the only one who knows
About this spiritual battle that lies within my addiction
that he and the devil agreed on
Like with Job no fiction
Addiction is the devils touchdown of spiritual warfare
gain a faithful relationship with god to truly understand how much he cares
feeling helpless while continuing to self destruct our minds
the key to overcome darkness is to move forward and leave the rest behind
Patients is the number one key
Just live life and be all that you can be
Follow the light be positive and place all negative dark energy on the shelf
Be a better person and start working on bettering your self.

CYNTHIA A. THOMAS

EMPTY

!EMPTY!
LIKE A FULL GLASS OF ICE COLD WATER THAT HAS BEEN
DEVOURED AND TOSSED AWAY
!EMPTY!
LIKE A FULL HOUSE FILLED WITH FAMILY LOVE AND
HAPPINESS BUT NO LONGER AND NOW
ABANDON AND QUIET
!EMPTY!
LIKE A MOTHERLESS,FATHERLESS CHILD LEFT ALONE TO
MANEUVER THROUGH THIS ICE COLD WORLD ALONE
!EMPTY!
LIKE A HEART THAT WAS ONCE COMPETENT BUT NOW
DESTROYED AND SHATTERED INTO A MILLION STONES
!EMPTY!
LIKE A PROSTITUTE DIRTY WHORE NUMEROUS SEXUAL
ENCOUNTERS WITH EACH ONE TAKING A CHUNK OUT OF
HER WHICH HAS LEFT HER
!EMPTY!
LIKE A FEMALE SLAVE WHO HAS JUST GIVEN BIRTH ONLY
TO HAhVE HER BABY TAKEN AWAY AND SOLD
!EMPTY!

CYNTHIA A. THOMAS

I'M FREE

I didn't know how good it would feel to be free, no worries , no stress and no
pain. Thank the Lord I'm free.
Sorry, if I hurt anyone as I pass through this journey called life,
I did the best that I could, and I put up a great fight.
A fight with my demons who came to devour my soul
I fought until the death of me yet only my God knows
that the pain that I endure has finally gone away Look for me in the clouds
My spirit is there and it's safe
So don't cry, my child I'm with God and this will be my new place
I'm free, no more pain and I will be with you always..

CYNTHIA A. THOMAS

FAMINE OF LOVE

Loving you is like chewing glass.
Each bite gets more painful than the last bite pressure being applied to my
inner cheeks causing mini brutal slashes resulting in blood flowing
similar to a river, more less a creek.
It's making me sick just like loving you it's like the consequences of chewing
glass causes me to scream out in Agony just like your love.
It's like releasing the chewed up glass through my bowels.
bloody pieces of glass exits my ass landing into the Commode
Like your love it's a waste
flushed away
My mom asked me about our love and I try to explain it
I told her loving you was like chewing glass
I would rather starve in a famine.

CYNTHIA A. THOMAS

WIFE CONFESSION

Wish you could understand that I so desperately want to be that woman
that you need me to be but life has taken a toll on me see
It's so hard for me to break loose of these feelings of despair, sadness and de-
pression. Pray that the Lord sends me this one particular blessing
to be free and fly away like a bird in the sky
to one day never cry
forgive me my love I'm not in control or at least that's how I feel
Every day I wake up its hate, hate, kill, kill
Forgive me my love I want to get it together
at night that's what I tell myself
but in the morning is like whatever
Forgive me my love what I do have is hope that the sun will shine
and I'll gravitate towards a piece of a sound mind.

CYNTHIA A. THOMAS

ADDICTED

What other explanation is there but I'm addicted
Mentally enslaved some what like a prisoner restricted

Coming out of my mothers womb was the worst pain I've ever felt.
At the age of five I was molested, that was the worst hand I was ever dealt.

Repeating the same cycle was something I said I would never do.
They say what goes around comes around. I had to learn the hard way that
that statement was true.

True that I sat down and witnessed what self destruction does.
I joined the self-destruct thinking I would gain
some love.

What better explanation is there but I'm addicted.

Addicted to the pain that I caused myself ,
pain was something that was normal
while being at peace was something I've never felt.
A dream that I hope one day will become
reality.
I'm addicted to disrespect, addicted to self hate and lack of morality.
What better explanation is there but I'm addicted

CYNTHIA A. THOMAS

A LETTER FROM YAHWEH

Just imagine you are a parent with a child as beautiful as the moon
Can you remember the first time that child held their first spoon?
You love that child more than ever and showered that child with
more than they could imagine?
And that child cursed you in an orderly fashion
"I don't need you even though you are giving me all that I need"
My child I love you and want the best for you so why can't you see it?
My heart is pure and I want the same for you
My child, the way you live your life you're DOOM!!
temptation is worse than ever and evil is lurking you need me to be
your shield and protect you for certain
all I ever wanted is to give you peace and freedom from within
but you ignore me It's sort of like not being able to see the wind
you just know it's there "why won't you love me the way
I love and care for you?"
"Why the lack of acknowledgement?" It's me Yahweh I'm the TRUTH!!

CYNTHIA A. THOMAS

AFTERLIFE

Where do we go when we die? What do we feel at that moment ? Does it
feel fake or does it feel real? Are we moving? Or are we still?
Da After life!
Could it be scary because of the unknown?
Are we alone or with others? Or Does it feel as if we're sound asleep like a
baby cuddled up under their mother ?
Da After life!
Most including myself, take life for granted, then once we make it to the oth-
er side, most likely we will regret it
I do know that I want to be at peace when I'm dead gone, and deceased.
Da Afterlife!!!!

CYNTHIA A. THOMAS

MY HEART

Where should I start mmm let's start with my heart
It's like someone placed it in the middle of the highway during rush hour
Being crushed ran over smashed as well as devoured
Where should I start? Mmm Let's start with my heart which has
vanished without saying goodbye
Haven't seen a day that was fulfilling yet
"Be patient have faith live life with no regrets" they advised
Ok how about my heart it has been shattered to pieces
The pain never slow down in fact it keeps on increasing
So miss me with that talk about this and that
Guarantee you can't walk a mile in my shoes hunny trust and believe that
that's a damn fact!

CYNTHIA A. THOMAS

LOST

Lost......... What does it mean when he or she is lost?
Lost in the mind? Lost within your spirit? Lost of what?
Maybe it's when a person is unsure of who he or she might be
If that's what it is, then maybe that's me!!
Who am I? A person who don't give a damn about anyone or anything
I'm a person who goes on day-to-day just daydreaming.
Ever since I was a little girl I would daydream
Daydream about happiness, and how it will truly feel to be joyful
Daydream about a miracle that I felt will never come.
LOST

CYNTHIA A. THOMAS

FATAL REACTION

Not making excuses for my actions but my life has been hell since
I was born that's my fatal reaction
when people sit and gossip about me they say "what's wrong with her, is she
blind dumb or insane"
I say fux you cause you don't know my pain
you have not walked in shame with people pointing their fingers,
But who is to blame !!! I made a decision to live the way I live
they say forget about the past move on and just live
learn how to forgive
because it is what it is
molested segregated from my mother at the age of two
no one gave me love
instead they replaced it with abuse
Until
I realize that my skin
had to be thicker than what it was
I
Learn to live and forgive I learn true meaning of self love

CYNTHIA A. THOMAS

A DIFFERENT GIRL

So what if they talk about you assuming you are oblivious to the
fact that you are different
Different In the way you view life, but hold on just listen
To the fact that you should rejoice and celebrate that you were
given a enormous purpose
Things could be worse than what they are keep pushing it will be worth it
So don't feel disappointed hold your head and rejoice
God created you uniquely molding you to be his voice
When creating someone special who unknowingly will change the world
Live your life with a purpose, you're an amazing
DIFFERENT GIRL!!

CYNTHIA A. THOMAS

MOTHERLESS & CRACK

Motherless so empty inside, lonely and angry are the feelings that run
through that child's body why? Why must I feel so sorry?
My children are feeling the same pain so yeah that's a damn shame.
I must be the dumbest person in the world
to put my kids through what I've been through as a little girl
Only God knows that I am lost and I'm blind what's going on?
only God knows that I've lost my mind, it's totally gone!
God will it ever come back? No my child because you're addicted to crack
, just like your mother an addict
you said you never be like her
You want the the truth here it goes have it
Molested, homeless, prostitution the story goes on and on
Question... When are you going to stop singing that same old song?
Darling open up your eyes and get it together.
If not, your life is going to be hell forever and ever.

CYNTHIA A. THOMAS

HUMAN IN THE MIRROR

Go away now you dumb motherfucker
I hate you with a passion you ain't shit but a sucker
Afraid to discover the inner core of who you are
So you wear a mask so no one can tell
Who and why you
are binge drinking at bars
Chasing death Because it seems that's your only escape
From reality from the truth you ain't shit but a fake
Human in the mirror I want to adore you but don't no how
There's pain agony and despair behind that beautiful smile
Which transforms itself into hate and anger
Human in the mirror where is the self discipline why so obsessed with danger
Want to die but afraid to pull the trigger
So you put yourself in situations to be taken out each situation you aim big-
ger and bigger Human in the mirror what a cowardly move
get it together life can
Be hard weather the storms staying positive is a awesome way to start

CYNTHIA A. THOMAS

NAIVE CONFIDENCE

Lol naïve confidence and foolish perception
Once insecure couldn't understand his rejection
So you made your face up painted your lips
you whore tight pants to show off your hips
All of the attention you receive made, you feel loved and wanted
The other girls were jealous. They talked about you and taunted.
They taunted the fact that you're obviously insecure,
oblivious to the fact that self love is the damn cure.
LOL YUP NAIVE CONFIDENCE

CYNTHIA A. THOMAS

JEALOUS

Jealous?

Of the way I saunter the twist in my hips

Or is it the shift of my lips?

Jealous?

Of the way I adore my consciousness

Or are you jealous of the men salivating over my fuselage muttering to their

homeboys that i'm perfected

Jealous?

Of the way I consummate my words

How I respect my uniqueness

Knowing my merit and what I deserve

Jealous?

As I wither through life ndazed

Mmmmm I would be to if I told you my secret on how I'm near perfection

You would laugh and say "girl you're a fool"

Jealous??

Hold up let me ask you again

Jealous??

NO TITLE

No matter what you say God always make a way to show us his true love
to show us that we should stay
on the path of righteousness, to be happy and free
. No one understands how hard this journey of life will be
for us to get to the light and out of darkness,
but with faith and faith alone, we can make it through this regardless
we could turn away from the wrong things in life
and start moving towards the right
nothing good comes in life trust me nothing good comes without a fight
anything easy is mediocre and trust me that's not good
and if you come where I come from
that statement should be understood
Let's take this journey together and love one another
let's stop being scared like a abuse child hiding from her abuser cowardly
under the covers
First Remove shame, second guilt and third fearfulness
jump up and rejoice God is the way summit and be filled with bliss!!

CYNTHIA A. THOMAS

BLACK EYES

Big red nose. giant feet, unique attire, and fancy cars
Standing there with the enemy without a care
Following orders which destroys your people doing what you are told so that
your master will
Keep you
Up under his wing safe and protected
number one requirement is to deliver his message
That will destroy generations after generations
You should be ashamed of yourself, but yet you sit in there celebrating
Life, like you have not done anything wrong,
you have full responsibility people look up to you and your songs
go against Illuminati for the sake of mankind
I'm talking about the celebrities and I have plenty of reasons
You are a waste of breath might
Be better off not breathing
With those black
Eyes

CYNTHIA A. THOMAS

KHAI
HEART
JU

My heart and my inspiration are my children
I never want them to go where I have been
Like when I was scheming and hustling with no self control and no self
discipline
I want them to be the best that they desire to be
To believe in the lord because the lord will set them free
When things get tough to pray have strong faith and believe
That they must take the good with the bad
Don't give up, stay strong
Hold your head high moving through this world standing firm and tall.

CYNTHIA A. THOMAS

UNBEKNOWNST CHANGED

I was once that chick, who was loyal, and would die before she snitched.
Who once was adventurous with plenty of friends
I was happy deep down, but then everything all changed
except for my name oh yea that shit stayed the same
Relocated my place of residence which was different and
I even had another child
as a young lady foolishly in love wow,
to make matters worse my self-respect was mild
growing up I was sexually abused I tried to love myself,
but I figure what's the use.
Nobody else loves me so I continued the abuse on myself,
More so on my body and everything that came along with it
I am a split image of my mom, and how did I deal with it ?
drinking and smoking which seemed to dull the pain
Mentally I was lost idiotically thinking I was sane
I started to pray to God that's when he provided me
with the willingness to change
Its not where we start but it's definitely how we finish.
Our life is not over,If we gain the strength to fight
We can start over with a fresh new beginning

CYNTHIA A. THOMAS

THE PLOTT

The food that we eat is killing us see
its the reason why we have organ failure
the reason why we can't be all that we can be you thought it was OK to have
section 8,
but trust me it came with a price that we can
Not afford to pay
the government is not your friend he's the enemy stop being so blind get off
social media so you can see
That we can't be all we can damn be if we stay blinded let's just stick together
let's be one-sided
they laugh at us as if we're a joke
we're just guinea pigs.
Their first experiment was blended with Coke.
Yea you remember the crack error
if we don't change our mentality, life won't get better.
They've been plotting on us from the beginning and I bet while reading this
bet you're saying "yeah whatever"
open up your eyes can't you see what's going on
Truth is I'm getting tired of us singing that same old song.
Called "ITS BECAUSE WE'RE BLACK"
type shit

CYNTHIA A. THOMAS

TWO FUX

No matter what anyone may say about me. It doesn't bother me too much
because deep down in my soul, I have faith that my father will rescue me
" she is this she is that oh yea so what!!
only god can judge me, so I really don't give two Fux
they say, it's not where you start its where you finish,
but honestly C.A.T has known that shit
from the beginning
sooner than later she will be laid to rest
dear father God guide my soul, as I go through life, lonely, and depressed

Milton Keynes UK
Ingram Content Group UK Ltd.
UKHW051107141024
449707UK00018B/225